PROMISES FROM GOD

STUDIES IN THIS SERIES *Available from your Christian bookstore*

promises
from God

8 DISCUSSIONS FOR GROUP BIBLE STUDY

MARILYN KUNZ &
CATHERINE SCHELL

TYNDALE HOUSE
PUBLISHERS, INC.
WHEATON, ILLINOIS

First printing, December 1988
Library of Congress Catalog Card Number 88-51602
ISBN 0-8423-4981-2
Copyright 1988 by Marilyn Kunz and Catherine Schell
Printed in the United States of America

contents

HOW TO USE THIS DISCUSSION GUIDE

This thematic study, *Promises,* is intended for use by adult discussion groups that have studied several books of the Bible using study guides in the Neighborhood Bible Studies series, and for church groups whose members are familiar with the Bible.

Church school teachers will find this study helpful in developing thoughtful discussion in their classes of senior highs and adults.

Some church groups, as well as Bible study groups that meet in homes, may wish to consider the sharing of leadership.

SHARING LEADERSHIP—WHY AND HOW

Each study guide in the Neighborhood Bible Studies series is prepared with the intention that an adult group or a senior high group, by using this guide, will be able to rotate leadership of the discussion. Those who are outgoing in personality are more likely to volunteer to lead first, but within a few weeks it should be possible for almost everyone to have the privilege of directing a discussion.

Reasons for this approach are:

(1) The discussion leader will prepare in greater depth than the average participant.

(2) The experience of leading a study stimulates a person to be a better participant in discussions led by others.

(3) When there is a different leader each week, group members tend to feel that the group belongs to everyone in it. It is not "Mr. or Mrs. Smith's Bible study."

(4) The more spiritually mature Christian with a wider knowledge of the Bible who is equipped to be a spiritual leader in the group is set free to *listen* to everyone in the group in a way that is not possible when leading the discussion. He (she) takes his regular turn in leading as it comes around, but if he leads the first study he must guard against the temptation to use a great deal of outside knowledge and source material that would make others feel they could not possibly attempt to follow his example of leadership.

For study methods and discussion techniques, refer to the first booklet in the series, *How to Start a Neighborhood Bible Study,* as well as to the following suggestions.

HOW TO PREPARE TO PARTICIPATE IN A STUDY USING THIS GUIDE

(1) During the week before the group meeting, read carefully the Bible portions listed for the next study, keeping in mind the theme of that study. Read in at least two translations if possible.

(2) After you read the Bible passages, study through each portion using the questions in this guide book. Make brief notes of particular discoveries you wish to share with the whole group.

(3) If you take a study section each day, you can cover the discussion preparation in easy stages during the week. Use it in your daily time of meditation and prayer, asking God to teach you what he has for you in it.

(4) Use the guide questions as tools to dig deeper into the Bible passages and to help you relate your discoveries to the study theme.

(5) Review the whole study before coming to the discussion. As *an alternative* to using this study in your daily quiet time, spend at least an hour to an hour and a half in sustained study once during the week, using the above suggestions.

HOW TO PREPARE TO LEAD A STUDY

(1) Follow the above suggestions on preparing to participate in a study. Pray for wisdom and the Holy Spirit's guidance.

(2) Familiarize yourself with the study guide questions until you are comfortable using them in the discussion.

(3) Try to get the movement of thought in the study so that you are able to be flexible in using the questions.

(4) Pray for the ability to guide the discussion with love and understanding.

HOW TO LEAD A STUDY

(1) Begin with a brief prayer asking God's specific help for your study together. If you find extemporaneous prayer difficult, think through and write out your prayer ahead of time. A thoughtfully written prayer asking for God's direction can be a great help to the group. You may ask another member of the group to pray if you have asked him (her) ahead of time.

(2) Read aloud the Bible portions by the sections under which questions are grouped in the study guide. It is not necessary for everyone to read aloud or for each to read an equal amount. Assign readers by thought units (paragraphs or larger sections).

(3) Guide the group to discover what the passages say by asking the discussion questions. Use the suggestions from the next section, "How to Encourage Everyone to Participate."

(4) As the group studies the Bible portions together, encourage each person to be straightforward in his (her) responses. If you are sincere in your responses to Scripture, others will tend to be also.

(5) Allow time at the end of the discussion to answer the summary questions, which help tie the whole study together.

(6) Bring the discussion to a close at the end of the time

allotted. Close in prayer, using the prayer written at the end of the study if you wish.

HOW TO ENCOURAGE EVERYONE TO PARTICIPATE

(1) It is helpful to have a number of Bible translations available in the group. Encourage people to read aloud from these different translations as appropriate in the discussion. Many translations have been used in preparation of this study guide.

Particular references have been made to a few by the following abbreviations: JB—*The Jerusalem Bible;* NEB—*The New English Bible;* NIV—New International Version; RSV—Revised Standard Version; TEV—*Good News Bible* (Today's English Version); TLB—*The Living Bible.*

(2) Encourage discussion by asking several people to contribute answers to a question. "What do the rest of you think?" or "Is there anything else that could be added?" are ways of encouraging discussion.

(3) Be flexible and skip any questions that do not fit into the discussion as it progresses.

(4) Deal with irrelevant issues by suggesting that the purpose of your study is to discover what is *in the Bible passages* as it relates to the topic of the discussion for the day. Suggest an informal chat about tangential or controversial issues after the regular study is dismissed.

(5) Receive all contributions warmly. Never bluntly reject what anyone says, even if you think the answer is incorrect. Instead, ask in a friendly manner, "Where did you find that?" or "Is that actually what it says?" or "What do some of the rest of you think?" Allow the group to handle problems together.

(6) Be sure you as the leader don't talk too much. Redirect those questions that are asked you to the group. The leader is to act as moderator. As members of a group get to know each other better, the discussion will move more freely.

(7) Don't be afraid of pauses or silences. People need time

to think about the questions and the passage. Try *never* to answer your own question—either use an alternative question or move on to another area for discussion.

(8) Watch hesitant members for an indication by facial expression or body posture that they have something to say, and then give them an encouraging nod or speak their names.

(9) Discourage overtalkative members from monopolizing the discussion by specifically directing questions to others. If necessary, speak privately to the overtalkative one about the need for discussion rather than lecture in the group, and enlist his (her) aid in encouraging all to participate.

INTRODUCTION

God's promises are part of the fabric of the universe, more certain than the rising of the moon and the setting of the sun. We may forget what we pledge, and make promises beyond our power to keep. The LORD does not forget, and he has the power to accomplish all that he says he will do.

And the LORD gave Solomon wisdom, as he promised him. (1 Kings 5:12)

Blessed be the LORD who has given rest to his people Israel, according to all that he promised; not one word has failed of all his good promise, which he uttered by Moses his servant. (1 Kings 8:56)

And behold, I send the promise of my Father upon you; but stay in the city, until you are clothed with power from on high. (Luke 24:49)

For all the promises of God find their Yes in him. That is why we utter the Amen through him, to the glory of God. (2 Corinthians 1:20)

Let what you heard from the beginning abide in you. If what you heard from the beginning abides in you, then you will abide in the Son and in the Father. And this is what he has promised us, eternal life. (1 John 2:24)

The Lord has promised good to me;
His word my hope secures;
He will my shield and portion be
As long as life endures.

When we've been there ten thousand years,
* Bright shining as the sun,*
We've no less days to sing God's praise
* Than when we first begun.*

John Newton (1725–1806)

DISCUSSION ONE
DEUTERONOMY 29–30
THAT YOU MAY PROSPER

The people of Israel are about to enter the land that the LORD God promised them forty years before when he brought them out of slavery in Egypt. In spite of their miraculous deliverance from Pharaoh's armies, the Israelites had refused to trust the LORD to go before them and to give them this land. Then, forbidden to enter the land, they wandered in the desert until all that adult generation died.

Now, as the next generation stands in the land of Moab ready to enter the Promised Land, Moses reviews the covenant the LORD made with their parents at Mount Sinai (chapters 24–28). In chapters 29 and 30, Moses calls on the Israelites to renew this covenant to follow the LORD their God, to serve and obey him.

(In preparing for this discussion read straight through Deuteronomy 29–30, aloud if possible. Imagine yourself as one of those hearing Moses as he addresses the people of God.)

DEUTERONOMY 29:1-9

1. Of what does Moses remind the people of Israel concerning:
    - their escape from Egypt?
    - their forty years in the desert (wilderness)?
    - their victories in *this place?*

2. What have the people of Israel failed to understand about their past history? To what extent are you like the Israelites in this respect? Why is it easy to forget what God has done for us in the past?

3. What is the way to prosperity (success) for the people of God? What roads to prosperity do people try to follow today?

Note: Verse 9, *prosper*—may also be translated "thrive," "succeed," "deal wisely."

DEUTERONOMY 29:10-15

4. Describe this scene. What are the purposes of this gathering? What individuals and groups of people are included?

5. To whom had the LORD originally made the promise being fulfilled this day?

Note: *Covenant* (verse 9)—compact, contract, or agreement between two parties.

6. In addition to themselves, for whom do the people speak this day as they enter into their covenant with the LORD (verses 14-15, RSV, TEV)? What effects can godly ancestors have upon later generations? Consider the ways that you have been affected by past decisions of godly people in your family, your church, your community, your nation.

DEUTERONOMY 29:16-29

7. Against what sin does Moses specifically warn God's people? If Moses were giving this warning today, in what terms do you think he would state his warning? What gods do people serve today?

8. What will be the dire results (verses 19-21) if someone thinks he is safely included in the blessings of the covenant but stubbornly persists in going his own way?

Note: *sweeping away of moist and dry alike* (RSV), *disaster on the watered land as well as the dry* (NIV) (verse 10). A proverbial expression meaning total destruction.

9. What actions by the Israelites would mean breaking their covenant with the LORD, the God of their fathers? Compare verses 17-18, and 26.

10. If the LORD's people break their covenant with him, what will happen to their land and to them (verses 22-28)?

11. What will be the reaction of their descendants, and of other nations, to such judgment (verse 24)? How is it possible to break (forsake) the covenant of the Lord today?

12. Read verse 29 in several translations. Put it into your own words.

(If you wish to handle this study in two sessions, divide it at this point.)

DEUTERONOMY 30:1-10

(If you handle this study in two sessions, review briefly what was discovered in chapter 29 before beginning chapter 30.)

13. What three things are those who have experienced God's judgment to do (verses 1-2)? Compare these actions with those for which they were judged in 29:25-26.

14. When they have fulfilled his conditions, what does the LORD promise to do for his people, physically and spiritually (verses 3-9)?

15. Note the conditions repeated in verse 10. Why do you think the great promises of verses 3-9 are based on such conditions?

16. Think about what it means to "turn to the Lord with all your heart and with all your soul." How does this, or how would this, change your life?

DEUTERONOMY 30:11-20

17. What possible objections does Moses imagine that the people may have? What is his clear and simple answer (verse 14)?

18. List in two columns the basic choices presented and the promised results.

19. Imagine yourself as one of the people present when Moses spoke. What are your thoughts, your reactions?

Summary

1. Review the promises (for good and for evil) and their conditions in these two chapters.

2. How does loving and obeying God become a part of one's daily experience? In what ways are you seeking to prosper spiritually?

Prayer

O Lord, make us aware of the implications of the choices we make today, and every day. Make us sensitive each day to how we follow either a pattern of obedience or of disobedience to your will. Deliver us from the delusion that anything or anyone except you will satisfy the deepest longings of our heart. Grant that the life and blessings we choose may affect for good not only our generation but those who come after us. We pray this in Jesus' name. Amen.

Memorize

And we desire each one of you to show the same earnestness in realizing the full assurance of hope until the end, so that you may not be sluggish, but imitators of those who through faith and patience inherit the promises. (Hebrews 6:11-12, RSV)

DISCUSSION TWO
2 KINGS 22; 23:1-30
DISASTER DELAYED

Josiah comes to the throne of Judah in 640 B.C. at the age of eight, when his father, Amon, is assassinated. Josiah's grandfather, Manasseh, during his long reign had led the nation into apostasy and rebellion against the LORD, and Amon continued on the same path. Now Assyria's power is weakening, and there is opportunity to turn Judah away from depending on Assyria and its gods.

Reform involves change. Change is never easy, especially if such change means altering ingrained patterns of thought and behavior, and setting new goals for one's attitudes and actions. During his thirty-one year reign, Josiah seeks to reverse the course set for the nation of Judah by Manasseh and Amon.

(In preparation for this study, read from 22:1–23:30 before starting detailed study of individual sections.)

2 KINGS 22:1-13

1. What do you learn about Josiah from verses 1-2? What does he initiate in the eighteenth year of his reign? How do you imagine this project would affect the young people in Judah? What kind of person does Josiah seem to be as suggested by the orders he gives (verses 4-7)?

2. What discovery is made during the repairs on the house of the LORD? How does King Josiah react when he hears what the Book of the Law says? What actions does he take? Compare with responses to the Scriptures that you observe people making today.

Note: Verse 8, *the Book of the Law*—very likely the Book of
Deuteronomy, or a major portion of it (see Discussion
1), since Josiah's reforms relate so closely to its
contents.

2 KINGS 22:14-20

3. What message does Huldah the prophetess have from
the LORD? Why is the LORD going to bring disaster upon
Jerusalem and its people? What special message does Huldah
have for Josiah? What attitude and actions of his are
commended?

4. How does Josiah respond to God's message? What
promise is given him because of his penitence? Josiah is
described (verse 9, in various translations) as *tender,
responsive, penitent of heart, sorry, concerned,* and *humbled
before the LORD.* What do you think that it means to *humble
yourself before the Lord?*

2 KINGS 23:1-3

5. Describe this scene. Whom does Josiah call together to
hear the reading of the book of the covenant?

What actions does the king take to bring reformation? What
solemn promises does he make in his *covenant before the
LORD?*

6. What effect does hearing all the book of the covenant
have upon the people? How do they respond to Josiah's
leadership?

How is the Word of God listened to and responded to in
your church? What would help to give public Scripture
reading greater impact in your church? How can each of us
renew our commitment to the commands of the LORD?

2 KINGS 23:4-14

7. List all the ways that false religions have gained a foothold among the people of Judah (verses 4-14). In each instance what actions does Josiah take to correct the situation?
Note: Verse 4, *Baal*—god of fertility worshiped by the
Canaanites whose female counterpart was *Asherah,*
represented by a wooden image. *Host of heaven* or
stars—the Assyrians worshiped the planets and stars.
Verse 13, *Ashtoreth* (Astarte)—a mother goddess of
fertility, love, and war, worshiped by the Canaanites;
Chemosh—sacrifice of children as burnt offerings was a
part of his worship; *Milcom*—a Canaanite god.

8. What had those who were in leadership before Josiah done to lead the people into worship of false gods (verses 5, 11-13)?

9. What possible headlines might have appeared in the *Jerusalem Post* if the newspaper had existed in Josiah's day?

2 KINGS 23:15-23

10. What drastic action does Josiah take as he continues to remove places of heathen worship even from part of the former territory of Israel? Whose tomb does he preserve and why?

11. After destroying all the places of idol worship, what does the king command the people to do (verse 21)? How is this Passover compared to previous celebrations?
Note: *Passover*—the festival recalls the Israelites' deliverance
from bondage in Egypt. After a series of plagues, the
angel of death passed over the homes on whose
doorposts had been sprinkled the blood of a sacrificial
lamb. In all other homes in Egypt, the firstborn son
died. The reaction to this disaster moved Egypt's
Pharaoh to allow the Israelites under Moses' leadership

to depart from the country. A meal of lamb and unleavened bread celebrated the event.

2 KINGS 23:24-30

12. What does Josiah get rid of in order to follow the words of the law of God? What *mediums* and *wizards (spiritists)* and *idols* exist in our society today?

13. Consider how a summary of your life might read. What would be included in what you wanted to *establish* and what you wanted to *put away*?

14. What attitudes and actions make Josiah unique? Compare Deuteronomy 6:4-5.

Summary

1. In what ways did those in power before Josiah lead the people to break the first two of the Ten Commandments that God had given them? (See Exodus 20:3-4.)

2. How did Josiah try to renew the commitment of his people to the promises the nation had made to the LORD when it was founded under Moses' leadership?

3. What can we do to emulate Josiah's concern for the things of God and his willingness to take action against spiritual evil? How do you think that renewal can be brought about in your church? What areas in your own life need improvement?

Prayer

O Lord, renew a right spirit within us. Deliver us from spiritual lethargy. Help us to serve you with an eager heart, renewing our promises and commitment to serve you all our days. In Jesus' name, we pray. Amen.

Memorize

Let us hold fast the confession of our hope without wavering, for he who promised is faithful; and let us consider how to stir up one another to love and good works. (Hebrews 10:23-24, RSV)

DISCUSSION THREE
JEREMIAH 32:26-44; 33
ENCOURAGEMENT FOR A PRISONER

Assyria, which conquered the northern kingdom of Israel almost a century before the time of Jeremiah, is losing power over its vast empire, and Babylon will soon take control of the Middle East. Jeremiah warns the kingdom of Judah of coming disaster. In spite of the determined efforts of King Josiah to bring reform, and Jeremiah's appeals, the people of Judah are hopelessly enmeshed in idolatry and will not give it up.

Though Jeremiah began his ministry as a prophet in 626 B.C. during the reign of Josiah (Discussion 2), these two chapters are dated in Zedekiah's reign forty years later, a short time before the final collapse of Jerusalem in 586 B.C. Jeremiah now seeks to prepare Jerusalem to face the Babylonian invasion. Because he is seen as pro-Babylonian, Jeremiah is confined to the Court of the Guard in the royal palace of Judah on orders of King Zedekiah. In 32:16-25, Jeremiah has asked the LORD why he instructed him to purchase a field and register the deed if the city will soon be handed over to the Babylonians. This study deals with the LORD's answer to the prophet's question.

(Before you begin to study the sections covered by the questions in this discussion, read all of chapters 32 and 33.)

JEREMIAH 32:26-44

1. How does the LORD identify himself (verse 27)? In what situations can you imagine that these words might be addressed to you? Wht would your answer be?

2. What terrible things are going to happen to Jerusalem? Why?

25

3. What groups of people does the LORD indict? List all the terrible things that they have done to arouse the LORD's anger and wrath (verses 29-35).

What activities in present day society do you think might bring a similar reaction from the LORD?

4. How does the LORD describe the way they have insulted him (verse 33)? Using phrases from this verse, how would you describe your attitude toward God?

5. To what atrocities has their idol worship led the people of Judah?

6. Though God is handing Jerusalem over to the Babylonians in judgment, what promise does he make (verses 28-29, 36-37)?

7. List all the promises God makes in verses 37-41. Contrast the relationship described in verse 33 with that in verses 38-40.

8. From verses 39-40, what do you think it means to *fear* God? Why is it dangerous to have no fear of God? How do you think that we can help our children to have a proper fear of God?

9. What are God's intentions for his people (verses 40-41)?

10. What promises in verses 42-44 are as sure as the LORD's judgments in verses 28-29?

JEREMIAH 33:1-13

11. How does Jeremiah's physical situation contrast with the way the LORD identifies himself and with what he promises Jeremiah (verses 2-3)?

What situations in your life have imprisoned you? Why do we sometimes fail to call on the Lord and then complain that he doesn't seem to hear us?

12. What has already happened, and what will yet happen in Jerusalem (verses 4-5)? Why is the city in such straits?

13. What does God promise he will do for his people

(verses 6-8)? How will these events affect the attitude of other nations toward the LORD (verse 9)?

14. Contrast the two descriptions of *the cities of Judah and the streets of Jerusalem* in verses 10 and 11. Where will the celebration take place? What message will be sung?

15. What additional promises does the LORD make in verses 12-13?

Note: These prophecies were fulfilled in the return of exiles to Judah and Jerusalem after seventy years in Babylonian captivity.

JEREMIAH 33:14-26

16. What promises to his people does the LORD guarantee in verses 14-16? Contrast the future quality of life in Judah and Jerusalem with that in 32:29-35 for which God will soon judge them.

17. What is the covenant which the LORD made with David and with the Levites who minister as priests before him (verses 17-18)?

18. To what other sure covenant does the LORD refer in order to show the certainty of his promises to David and the Levitical priests, and to the descendants of Abraham, Isaac, and Jacob (verses 20-26)?

19. Read Luke 1:31-33 and Hebrews 9:11-12, 24-26. How does Jesus Christ fulfill the promises of Jeremiah 33:17-18?

Summary

1. What three major emphases do you observe in this section of Jeremiah?

2. What is revealed here about the character of God? about his power? about his control over history?

3. What difference does this make in your life?

Prayer

O Lord, how often we limit what you can do in our lives because we think and act as if some things are "too hard" for you. Forgive us! Help us to believe your Word that your promises are as certain of fulfillment as the regular coming of day and night. Help us to hate evil and to love righteousness so that we may be your people and you will be our God. We pray in the name of Jesus, Son of David, our High Priest and King. Amen.

Memorize

Then the word of the LORD came to Jeremiah: "I am the LORD, the God of all mankind. Is anything too hard for me?" (Jeremiah 32:26-27, NIV)

Since promises are good only if one can depend on the faithfulness and power of the one who makes them, this psalm about God's dealings with his people is important to us.

As you read Psalm 107, notice the structure of this lyric poem: an introduction followed by four word-pictures of difficult human situations and the LORD's interventions, then a description of reversals God brings about in the affairs of mankind, and a concluding reminder to apply what has been learned to one's own life.

(Read the whole psalm aloud before you study it in detail. Notice the words and phrases the poet uses to stir your emotions.)

PSALM 107:1-3

1. Who ought to give thanks to the LORD? For what reasons?

Note: Verse 2, *redeemed*—the Hebrew word expresses the right of the next of kin to intervene and rescue a relative in trouble, including paying a redemption price. (It expresses the right to rescue rather than an obligation to do so.)

2. "You know that you were ransomed from the futile ways inherited from your fathers, not with perishable things such as silver or gold, but with the precious blood of Christ. . . ." (1 Peter 1:18-19, RSV)

"God so loved the world that he gave his only Son, that

29

whoever believes in him should not perish but have eternal life." (John 3:16, RSV)

What do these New Testament quotations add to your understanding of what it means to be *redeemed?*

PSALM 107:4-9

3. Describe the experiences of these people. Today who experiences similar deprivation physically? emotionally?

4. What do these needy people lack, and how does God help them? Imagine what it is like not to have a home. How can you make your home a place where people are delivered from distress?

5. How may spiritual hunger and thirst be good things? Compare verse 9 with John 6:35 and Matthew 5:6.

PSALM 107:10-16

6. What colors would you use to paint a picture of this scene? If you were to act it out in dance, what movements and body postures would you use? What situations in life illustrate *doors of bronze* or *bars of iron?*

7. What actions have led to the depression and distress described here? Read verse 11 in several translations.

Give an example of someone spurning *the counsel of the Most High.* How can we be sure to recognize his counsel?

8. When do the people described here receive help? What should be their response?

9. How can darkness and gloom be removed? Share, if you wish, an experience you have had of such relief from distress.

PSALM 107:17-22

10. What caused the condition of the people described in verses 17-18? What are people doing today that may lead to similar consequences?

11. When and how are these sufferers delivered? Give an example of an instance when you found the Word of God to be powerful in your life. Read Hebrews 4:12.

12. What three actions are appropriate responses to the LORD's healing and deliverance? Give examples of such responses today. How do you thank the LORD?

PSALM 107:23-32

13. Using this section make an outline for a talk about the ups and downs, storms, and stresses people face in the business world. What points would you emphasize?

14. How does God deliver (verses 29-30)? What responses are appropriate? Describe how one could fulfill the commands in verses 31-32.

15. Share examples of the LORD helping you in your work.

PSALM 107:33-43

16. What caused the problems in verses 33-34? Contrast these two verses with verses 35-38. How are some lands today no longer suitable for growing food because of what people have done? Give examples also of the opposite.

What do you see when you consider these verses as descriptions of poverty and riches of the mind and spirit?

17. What contrasting treatment does God give the powerful and the poor? What is the reaction of the upright? of the wicked?

18. What is the wise person to do?

Summary

1. Review Psalm 107 by tracing this pattern as you see it repeated in verses 4-32:
   - distressing situation
   - cry to the Lord for help

- what the Lord does to deliver
- appropriate response

2. What have you learned in this psalm about God?

3. In what situations have you been most aware of God's love?

Prayer

Lord, we praise you for your steadfast love, your great mercy, your power to deliver. Thank you for your patience and kindness to those in trouble because of foolishness and disobedience. Thank you for delivering those who cry to you for help. Let our words, our attitudes and actions, be an expression of praise for all that you are and all that you have done for us. We pray through Jesus Christ our Lord. Amen.

Memorize

O give thanks to the Lord, for he is good;
  for his steadfast love endures for ever!
Let the redeemed of the Lord say so,
  whom he has redeemed from trouble....
Let them thank the Lord for his steadfast love,
  for his wonderful works to the sons of men!
For he satisfies him who is thirsty,
  and the hungry he fills with good things.
(Psalm 107:1-2, 8-9, RSV)

Jesus' Sermon on the Mount is the essence and summary of
the teachings he gave to his disciples. The word *taught* in 5:2
is a verb form indicating habitual action: "this is what he used
to teach them." The sections chosen for this study cover the
beginning and ending of Matthew's collection of the official
teaching of Jesus.

MATTHEW 5:1-12
Introduction to Jesus'
Sermon on the Mount

   1. Read aloud from three translations these promises
called the Beatitudes. As you read or listen, be alert to the
different shades of meaning expressed in these different
versions.
Note: The word here translated *blessed* or *happy* describes
        the joy that does not depend upon the changing
        circumstances of life.
   2. How would you state the opposite of verse 3? Put into
your own words the meaning of "poor in spirit" and
"kingdom of heaven." Name other kingdoms that people
seek to possess today.
Note: In the Aramaic language, which Jesus spoke, the word
        poor describes the humble person who, because he or
        she is without any earthly resources, puts complete
        trust in God.
   3. Who is promised the comfort of the Lord? What is the

result if one is sorry for sin? Compare verse 4 with Psalm 51:15-17.

4. Compare verse 5 with Psalm 37:1-2, 9-11. With whom are the *meek* (*humble,* TEV) contrasted? What is promised to the meek?

Note: The word *meek* means to be humble before God, and because one is under God's control, to be in control of all of one's passions.

5. Why do you think that restlessness and dissatisfaction characterize the life of many men and women today? How does verse 6 redirect our search for satisfaction?

6. What does the Apostle Paul's personal testimony in Philippians 3:7-9 add to your understanding of what it means to *hunger and thirst for righteousness?*

7. What opportunities to be merciful have you had this week? What other reactions would have been possible?

8. See Luke 6:32-36 for more of Jesus' teaching on what it means to be merciful. Why should a Christian be merciful? By what standard are we to measure the degree to which we show mercy to others?

9. What is the reward of the *pure in heart?* See also 1 John 3:2-3. From Psalm 24:3-4, what do you think are the attitudes and actions of one who is pure in heart?

10. Read Titus 1:15-16. With whom are the pure contrasted? What happens to the minds and consciences of those who are not pure? How do such people tend to act?

11. What name is promised to those who are *peacemakers?* Describe a situation where someone you know was a peacemaker. What may it cost to be the person who makes peace in a troubled situation?

12. How do the last two beatitudes (verses 10-12) differ from the others? In what ways will Jesus' followers suffer? What does Jesus promise those who suffer for righteousness? In what honored company do those belong who are mistreated for Christ's sake?

13. What should be our response to such persecution? Do you take advantage of your opportunities to identify yourself as a follower of Christ? How?

MATTHEW 7:24-28
Conclusion to Jesus'
Sermon on the Mount

14. What does the person in verses 24-25 have in common with the one in verses 26-27? In what ways do they differ? Why is "hearing" Jesus' message not enough? What will happen if we do not act on the truth we hear?

15. Why do you think that Jesus concludes his sermon with this warning and this promise?

Summary

1. Compare the message in 5:1-12 with that in 7:24-28. How are they the same? How do they differ?

2. How do these passages help you to set goals for your life? How do they help you to prepare to meet the storms of life?

Prayer

Lord, make me aware of the opportunities you give me for happiness. Help me to remember in traffic and in the market checkout line that these are opportunities to exercise meekness and mercy. Help me to be pure in heart when I read and when I think. Give me the desire and the skill to be a peacemaker in my home and in my community. If I am reviled or persecuted, may it be only because of my faithfulness to you, Lord Jesus. Amen.

Memorize

Enter through the narrow gate. For wide is the gate and broad is the road that leads to destruction, and many enter through it. But small is the gate and narrow the road that leads to life, and only a few find it. (Matthew 7:13-14, NIV)

In the hours before his arrest, Jesus shares his heart with his disciples. They are disturbed by his predictions of betrayal, of his departure, and of Peter's denial (13:21, 33, 38). Jesus now encourages them by the promise of his return and of the coming of the Counselor, the Holy Spirit.

Emphasizing the things that are important for them to remember, Jesus tells his disciples what they are to be and to do.

(As you meet together, read aloud chapters 14 and 15 before starting detailed study of individual sections. Assign to different readers the words of Thomas, Philip, and Judas—not Iscariot. Ask three other people to read Jesus' words in chapter 14, 15:1-17, and 15:18-27.)

JOHN 14:1-14

1. What commands and what promises does Jesus give his disciples in verses 1-4? List them.

2. Put Thomas's question into your own words. In his answer, what claims does Jesus make for himself in regard to man's approach to God and man's knowledge of God?

3. What does Philip apparently want? What lack of understanding does he reveal by his request?

4. In answering Philip, what questions does Jesus ask? What claim does Jesus make as to the source of his own words and works?

5. What promises does Jesus make to his disciples in verses 12-14? What qualifications does he place on these promises?

How do people today use certain names to help them? What do you understand Jesus means when he says, "Ask in my name"?

Note: Verses 13-14, *in my name*—his *name* represents all that Jesus is, his character, authority, and power.

JOHN 14:15-24

6. What will be the proof that Jesus' disciples love him? List all the things stated in verses 15-17 about the one the Father will send to the disciples at Jesus' request.

Note: Verse 16, the Greek word *parakletos* can be translated as "counselor," "advocate," "intercessor," "protector," "support."

7. Note each promise Jesus makes to his disciples in verses 18-23. What is the test which proves that one loves Jesus (verses 15, 21, 23)? How do Jesus and the Father respond to such love?

JOHN 14:25-31

8. What two things will the promised Holy Spirit do for those to whom the Father sends him?

9. If you were one of the disciples, what would you especially remember from what Jesus tells you in verses 27-31?

JOHN 15:1-5

10. Look carefully at the word picture Jesus uses here. What relationship does Jesus describe between himself, his Father, and his disciples?

Note: In the Old Testament, the *vine* symbolized the chosen people, Israel, which God took out of Egypt and planted in the Promised Land. Their failure to bear the fruit of obedience led to God's judgment and exile.

Here Jesus calls himself *the true vine* whose fruit will not disappoint the Father.

11. What do Jesus' words in verse 5, *apart from me you can do nothing,* mean in your life? What promise is implicit in this statement?

JOHN 15:6-17

12. Find the promises and warnings in verses 6-11. What do they emphasize? What is Jesus' recipe for joy?

13. What standard of love does Jesus set for all those who follow him (verses 12-17)? See also John 10:11.

14. To what privileged relationship does Jesus call his disciples? What is the difference here between a *servant* and a *friend?*

JOHN 15:18-27

15. How will *the world* treat those who serve Jesus? Why?

16. What responsibility do Jesus' disciples share with *the Counselor, the Spirit of truth* (verses 26-27)?

Summary

1. If you had only chapters 14 and 15 of John's Gospel as your Bible, what would you know about Jesus? his promises? what it means to be his followers?

2. From Jesus' teachings in these chapters, list at least six specific responsibilities of every Christian.

3. What changes will there be if you determine to follow Jesus' teachings wholeheartedly?

Prayer

Lord Jesus, thank you that you have revealed the Father to us and opened the way into his presence. Thank you for loving us so much that you died for us and that you call us friends. Be at home in our hearts as we make our home in you. Deliver us from fear and unbelief. Enable us to be your witnesses in our generation. Amen.

Memorize

His divine power has bestowed on us everything that makes for life and true religion, enabling us to know the One who called us by his own splendour and might. Through this might and splendour he has given us his promises, great beyond all price, and through them you may escape the corruption with which lust has infected the world, and come to share in the very being of God. (2 Peter 1:3-4, NEB)

DISCUSSION SEVEN
1 CORINTHIANS 15:1-28, 35-58
DEATH IS DESTROYED!

Everyone faces death, sooner or later—the death of those we love and our own death. Paul's words on this subject to first century Christians at Corinth (in what is now Greece) challenge and comfort us today. In the questions Paul raises and answers, he speaks to issues that concern us as Christians.

1 CORINTHIANS 15:1-11

1. How had these people responded to the Good News (gospel) Paul preached to them (verses 1-2, 11)? What warning is implied in his promise in verse 2?

2. What message did Paul receive and pass on to the Corinthians? (Note the four statements introduced by *that* in verses 3-5.)

3. What six individuals and groups does Paul include in his list of witnesses to the Resurrection? How important to the gospel message does Paul seem to consider the fact of Christ's resurrection?

1 CORINTHIANS 15:12-28

4. Some of the Corinthians were saying that there is no resurrection of the dead. Trace Paul's argument in verses 12-19 by the *if* clauses in his answer.

Note: The Greeks believed that the soul was immortal and escaped from the body after death to continue a shadowy existence in the underworld or to be absorbed into the divine. To them physical resurrection was impossible.

41

5. What dire consequences follow for Christian believers if they deny the possibility of resurrection of the dead? Note in verses 17-19 how Paul makes this a personal issue.

How does Paul's clear statement that *Christ has been raised from the dead* answer the problems raised in verses 14, 17- 19?

6. List all the positive consequences of Christ's resurrection in verses 20-28. What sequence of events is promised?

Note: Verses 20-23 (RSV, NIV), *firstfruits*. On the day following the Sabbath after the Passover (the very day of Christ's resurrection), the first sheaf of the grain harvest was brought as an offering, consecrating and anticipating the full harvest.

7. What will happen to *the last enemy*? Compare verses 25-26 with Hebrews 2:14-15. What practical effect should Christ's victory over death have in our lives?

1 CORINTHIANS 15:35-50
(Read this section in RSV or NIV, and TEV or TLB.)

8. What two questions may some people have (verse 35)? How does Paul answer these questions? What illustrations from nature does he use (verses 36-44, 49)?

9. What clear promises are made in verses 42-44 as Paul describes how it will be when the dead are raised to life?

10. What contrasts does Paul draw between the first Adam and the last Adam (Christ)? List them in two opposing columns.

11. Verse 49 can be translated as a promise (*we shall*) or as an exhortation (*let us*). Compare with 1 John 3:2-3. In your own words, what does this mean? How should this affect the way we live?

1 CORINTHIANS 15:50-58

12. Since man's mortal physical body cannot inherit God's immortal kingdom (verse 50), what is going to happen? What transforming changes are promised at the last trumpet?
Note: The trumpet sometimes accompanies God's interventions in history. *The last trumpet* (verse 52) is the trumpet call announcing *the end* in verse 24.

13. When the events of verses 51-54 occur, what victory will be won?

14. How is death conquered, its sting drawn (verses 56-57)? Compare with Romans 4:25; 5:8-10.

15. What practical difference does Paul expect Christ's victory over death to make in the way Christians live (verse 58)?

Summary

1. Review Paul's list of witnesses who saw the risen Christ.

2. Because of the reality of the resurrection from the dead, what kind of life should a Christian lead here and now?

3. Review the promises in this chapter (verses 22-28, 49, 51-58). What difference do they make in your attitude toward death?

Prayer

Lord Jesus, you are our comfort and our hope. We find strength in your victory over death, knowing that we shall be like you when we too are raised from the dead. Thank you for your promise that we will be raised from death in a spiritual body of glory and power. Keep us firm and

43

steady all our life with the knowledge that we serve the One who is victor over sin and death. Thank you, Lord, that nothing we do in serving you is ever useless or in vain. Amen.

Memorize

For the Lord himself will come down from heaven, with a loud command, with the voice of the archangel and with the trumpet call of God, and the dead in Christ will rise first. After that, we who are still alive and are left will be caught up with them in the clouds to meet the Lord in the air. And so we will be with the Lord forever. Therefore encourage each other with these words. (1 Thessalonians 4:16-18, NIV)

The Book of the Revelation is the only book in the New Testament that describes the future at length. Most of the prophecies in the Old Testament have already been fulfilled in the coming of our Lord Jesus Christ, but much of this book has yet to be fulfilled. Here we see Jesus reigning in power and making all things right. In chapter 1, the writer is identified as *John,* a servant of God in exile on the island of Patmos *because of the word of God and the testimony of Jesus* (verse 9, NIV).

(Read aloud all of chapters 21 and 22 before starting to discuss individual sections. Ask readers ahead of time, using a different person for each paragraph unit. The leader for the day should decide which paragraph divisions to use if translations differ.)

REVELATION 21:1-8

1. Try to put yourself in John's place. What do you see and hear? How do you react to this experience?

Contrast the *new Jerusalem* with the earthly Jerusalem of Jeremiah 32:28-34 (Discussion 3).

2. What promises are announced by the voice from the throne (verses 3-4)? Compare with Isaiah 25:8. How does the one who sits upon the throne identify himself in verses 5-7?

3. In two opposing columns list the types of people who are contrasted in verses 6-8. What are they to receive?

4. *The cowardly, the faithless (unbelieving,* NIV; *those who break their word,* JB) are those who deny Christ because of

45

fear of man. See 2 Timothy 1:7 for the power available to the one who wants to *conquer* or *overcome* (21:7, RSV, NIV) and to be faithful.

REVELATION 21:9-21

5. What new things are shown to John? Describe the promised Holy City, its walls and its gates.

Note: The twelve jewels in the foundation of the city walls are thought to be representative of the stones in the breastplate of the Old Testament high priest (Exodus 28:17-21).

The measurements of the city given in multiples of twelve have obvious symbolism. The city with its vast size (about fourteen hundred miles long, wide, and high) serves to unite earth and heaven. A perfect cube, it recalls the shape of the Holy of Holies in King Solomon's ancient temple in Jerusalem (1 Kings 6:20).

6. What do the gates and the foundations of the city symbolize? What does this show about the city of God in relation to the Old and New Testaments?

REVELATION 21:22-27

7. List the things that will not be found in this city (verses 22-23). Why are these things unnecessary here?

8. Describe the activities and influence of the new Jerusalem. Who and what shall come into the city? Who and what shall never enter it? Compare verses 27 and 3:5.

REVELATION 22:1-7

9. Describe the scene in verses 1-2. Compare this with Genesis 2:8-10. What is the effect of the tree of life as described in Revelation 22?

10. What type of future is promised in verses 3-6? For the *curse* in verse 3, see Genesis 3:14-24.

How are the effects of the *curse* (food produced only through painful toil, separation from the tree of life and from the presence of God) overcome in the new Jerusalem?

11. What five things do you learn about the servants of the Lamb? Compare verse 4 with Psalm 17:15.

REVELATION 22:12-21

12. What warning is implied in verses 12-15? On what basis will people be judged? Contrast the two experiences in verses 14-15.

Note: Some manuscripts read "do his commandments" instead of "wash their robes." Verse 15, *dogs*— elsewhere in Scripture, participants in heathen worship.

13. What examples have you observed of people who *love and practice falsehood?* Why is all evil a form of falsehood? How does a *sorcerer,* a *fornicator,* a *murderer,* or an *idolater* practice falsehood? What about their beliefs and actions is a lie?

14. What is the invitation in verse 17? By whom and to whom is it extended? For where to obtain the free gift of the *water of life,* see 22:1, and John 4:10, 13-14; 7:37-39.

15. Against what does John warn those who hear his message? See Paul's words in 2 Corinthians 4:1-2.

16. With what wonderful promise does the book conclude (verses 7, 20)? Are you able to echo John's response, *Amen. Come, Lord Jesus?*

Summary

1. Review the promises in these two chapters. Which do you find most meaningful? Why?

2. What truths are emphasized in 22:7, 12, 20? See also 2 Peter 3:8-9.

Prayer

Lord, your promises are so great! Forgive us that our understanding and faith are so small. Deliver us from unbelief. Stretch our minds and spirits so that we may be fit for the things that you have promised to come. We would drink now of the water of life that you promise to those who ask you for it. Help us to accept your training now in our lives that we may serve you here and in the heavenly Jerusalem. Amen and amen!

Memorize

But you have come to Mount Zion, to the heavenly Jerusalem, the city of the living God. You have come to thousands upon thousands of angels in joyful assembly, to the church of the firstborn, whose names are written in heaven. You have come to God, the judge of all men, to the spirits of righteous men made perfect, to Jesus the mediator of a new covenant, and to the sprinkled blood that speaks a better word than the blood of Abel. . . . Therefore, since we are receiving a kingdom that cannot be shaken, let us be thankful, and so worship God acceptably with reverence and awe, for our God is a consuming fire. (Hebrews 12:22-24, 28, NIV)

NOTES

NOTES

NOTES

NOTES

NOTES

RECOMMENDED PROGRAMS
FOR SMALL GROUP DISCUSSION BIBLE STUDY

New Groups and Outreach Groups

Mark (recommended as first unit of study)
Acts
John, Book 1 (Chapters 1–10)
John, Book 2 (Chapters 11–21)
Romans
Four Men of God (Abraham, Joseph, Moses, David)
1 and 2 Peter (Letters to People in Trouble)
Genesis (Chapters 1–13)

Groups Reaching People from Non-Christian Cultures

Genesis (Chapters 1–13)
Mark
Romans
Four Men of God (Abraham, Joseph, Moses, David)
Philippians and Colossians (Letters from Prison)

Church Groups

Genesis (Chapters 1–13)
Matthew, Book 1 (Chapters 1–16)
Matthew, Book 2 (Chapters 17–28)
1 Corinthians (Challenge to Maturity)
2 Corinthians and Galatians (A Call for Help and Freedom)
1 and 2 Peter (Letters to People in Trouble)
Psalms and Proverbs
Four Men of God (Abraham, Joseph, Moses, David)
Bible Leaders Who Coped with Stress
Isaiah

Mission Concerns Groups

Luke
Acts
Ephesians and Philemon
The Coming of the Lord (1 and 2 Thessalonians, 2 and 3 John, Jude)
Romans
1 John and James

Advanced Groups

Courage to Cope
They Met Jesus (Eight Studies of New Testament Characters)
Hebrews
The Coming of the Lord (1 and 2 Thessalonians, 2 and 3 John, Jude)
Promises from God

Sunday School (Adult and older teens)

Matthew, Book 1 (Chapters 1–16)
Matthew, Book 2 (Chapters 17–28)
They Met Jesus (Eight Studies of New Testament Characters)
Courage to Cope
Set Free

Biweekly or Monthly Groups

They Met Jesus (Eight Studies of New Testament Characters)
Set Free
Courage to Cope
Psalms and Proverbs

How to Start a Neighborhood Bible Study

(A Guide to Discussion Study) is also available.

IF

—you have found this study worthwhile
—your group is interested in being in touch with others involved in Neighborhood Bible Studies
—you would be willing to have NBS put people in touch with you who move to your area from other parts of the country and wish to find a new group
—your area or church would like to sponsor an NBS seminar
—you would like to hear what other groups are doing
—you would like to share what has been happening in your Bible study group

LET US HEAR FROM YOU!

....

QUESTIONNAIRE

1. Our Bible study group has met together for _____ years.

2. There are _____ (number) people in our group.

3. Our group is made up of (men, women, men and women, couples).

4. We are a (neighborhood, office, church, _____) group. Describe something about your group: _____ _____

5. We meet _____ (how often) at _____ (place).

6. _____ percent of our group are studying the Bible for the first time as adults.

7. We have studied the following books of the Bible using NBS guides: _____ .

8. The best method for adding new people to our group has been _____ .

    _____ other group(s) have started from our group.

9. We take turns being the discussion leader for the week, increasing participation and learning. (yes)   (no)

10. Additional comments: _____ _____ _____

(Clip and send. You may use label below.)

....

To:
NEIGHBORHOOD BIBLE STUDIES, INC.
Dobbs Ferry, New York 10522-0222